High-Heeled Manners

High-Heeled Manners

If You Obey All the Rules, You'll Miss All the Fun

CONARI PRESS

First published in 2005 by Conari Press,

an imprint of Red Wheel/Weiser, LLC
York Beach, ME
With offices at:
368 Congress Street
Boston, MA 02210
www.redwheelweiser.com

Acknowledgements on page 62.
ISBN: 1-57324-222-5

Typeset in TheSans, SignPainter, Ogre, Parade, Pike, Cafe Mimi,
and Felt-Tip Woman by Jill Feron, FeronDesign

Printed in China
CC

11 10 09 08 07 06 05
  8 7 6 5 4 3 2 1

High-Heeled Manners offers etiquette from the time of yore to your time in the areas of

- friendship
- fashion
- dating and marriage
- and beauty.

Sprinkled throughout with trivia and tips, as well as quizzes to test your manners—and teach you to mind them—this book will have you toting charm on your arm along with the season's hottest handbag . . .

> *"Etiquette—a fancy word for simple kindness."*
> —ELSA MAXWELL,
> ELSA MAXWELL'S ETIQUETTE BOOK *(1951)*

"Sit properly . . .
the world isn't interested
in the color of your PANTS."

—A MOTHER IN *GRACE NOTES*

Pinkie-Wagging High Tea

Hosting a formal high tea sounds daunting, so don't do it. Opt for an interpretation of this British art form and invite your girlfriends over for an afternoon of girl talk and dainty sipping. Whether you go all out and polish up your tea service or just boil some water, the fun part here is to have an array of different teas to try, from exotic fruit-infused blends to simple herbal standbys. Make finger sandwiches and scones (or better yet, pick some up at a bakery). Play dress up and invite the girls to wear hats and pearls.

Test Your Chick Quotient

"To have good friends, you gotta be a good friend."

If your mother didn't tell you this, consider yourself notified. Or maybe you already know what it takes to be a chick's best friend. Take the test below to see how your friendship abilities rate.

1. Your girlfriend has not returned your calls after you've left her two messages. Do you

    a. Feel hurt and wait for her to call you back?

    b. Call her again and tell her you miss her?

2. Your girlfriend's date repeatedly brushes against you and boldly grabs your behind. Do you

a. Take him aside and tell him what a louse he is, but save your girlfriend the embarrassment?
b. Feign something is in your eye, take your friend aside and tell her the guy's a creep?

3. Your girlfriend gives you a truly horrible scarf for your birthday. Do you

a. Tell her flat out it's not you and ask if you can return it?
b. Wear it fondly when she's around?

4. Your girlfriend's had one margarita too many and begins to tango quite clumsily but lustily with a lounge lizard. Do you

a. Cheer them on and order another round?
b. Grab her by the ear and tell Godzilla she's got someplace to be?

Turn the page for the results.

The Results for Testing Your Chick Quotient

MOSTLY "A" ANSWERS: Go straight to the Girlfriend Hall of Shame.

MOSTLY "B" ANSWERS: You got it goin' on, sister, and you probably have a gaggle of die-hard chick friends to prove it.

HALF AND HALF: There's hope. You have what it takes but you get a little stuck sometimes. Rule of thumb: Follow your heart and consider what the best move is to support your girlfriends and foster their success and happiness. You can't go wrong with that.

"It is wise to apply the oil of refined politeness to the mechanism of friendship."

— COLETTE

Flower Power

Following is a veritable garden of blossoms and plants with their various meanings. Inscribe a card to your girlfriend identifying the significance of each bloom to decode your sentiments. For a truly special touch, write the note on parchment, roll it up, and secure it with a pretty ribbon.

Blues-busting Bouquet

CHRYSANTHEMUM: Hope
FREESIA: Calmness
GLADIOLA: Natural grace
JASMINE: Good wishes
RED GERANIUM: Comfort

You Lost Ten Pounds and Look Like a Goddess Bouquet

BIRD OF PARADISE: Exotic and wonderful
DELPHINIUM: Swiftness and light
HEATHER: Passion
PINK FLOWERS: Any variety, the color means perfection

Best Friends Forever Bouquet

FORGET-ME-NOTS: Keep me in your heart
PERIWINKLE: Promise
SUNFLOWER: Adoration, strength, longevity
ROSES: Love

And a Brownie Smile to You

Do you remember
the Three Brownie Bs,
the principles all Brownies
(Girl Scouts ages 5–8)
are taught to memorize?

1.
Be
Discoverers

2.
Be
Ready
Helpers

3.
Be
Friend-
Makers

SAY ANYTHING?

"If you haven't got anything nice to say
about anybody, come sit next to me."
—ALICE ROOSEVELT LONGWORTH

"Show me someone who never gossips,
and I'll show you someone
who isn't interested in people."
—BARBARA WALTERS

TIPS ON GOSSIPING

"Remember: people talk "stink"
about others because *they* have little
self-esteem. Rise above that."
—SHARI ILALAOLE'S MOTHER

"The real art of conversation
is not only to say the right thing in
the right place, but to leave unsaid the
wrong thing at the tempting moment."
—DOROTHY NEVILL,
BRITISH AUTHOR, SOCIAL HOSTESS

Shoo Fly Don't Bother Me

Ever set out for a fabulously fun night with the gals, only to have it spoiled by the arrival of some lecherous hangers-on of the male persuasion? Some of our chick friends have come up with creative ways of getting those overly persistent guys out of your hair (for the night, at least).

THE CRYING GAME

If you notice a shark circling your group, quickly grab a bar napkin and start "sobbing." We're talking loud, gut-wrenching sobs while your girlfriends pet and coo, "There, there." Girlfriends should join in on the wailing, grabbing more and more bar napkins for the inevitable nose blowing. Don't worry if the "sobbing" develops into hysterical laughter; it'll sound legit.

THE ONE-UP(WO)MANSHIP

When the unwelcome one tries to impress you with his manly accomplishments, insist on talking about your feats. No matter what he's done, you've done it first, more often, better, and with superior style. And so has your best girlfriend. Drag her into the conversation so that she can add lines like, "Oh, you've only done the climb once—what's wrong? Ya got scared?" (Make chicken sounds.) "Well goodness! Did you *crawl* over the finish line or what?" (Make dog pants.)

EMILY POST:
Never Short on Good Advice

"All women who have any clothes sense whatever
know more or less the type of things that are
their style—unless they have such an attack
of fashionitis as to be irresponsibly delirious."

*

"A conspicuous evidence of bad style that has
persisted through numberless changes in fashion
is the over-dressed and over-trimmed head."

"When in doubt, wear the plainer dress. It is always better to be under-dressed than over-dressed."

21

EMERGENCY FASHION TIPS
No Need to Call 911

Hem come loose and no thread in sight?
Try **masking tape or a stapler**.

✚

Bring your patent leather shoes
back to life with **petroleum jelly**.
Rub a pea-sized amount into the leather.

✚

Use a **black felt-tipped laundry marker** to cover
over cracks in black leather shoes or to cover a
light-colored stain on any black cloth.

✚

No, freezing your panty hose will not keep a run
from spreading, but **clear nail polish** will.

Miss Manners on Shopping

If you must use your cell phone, take it outside the store. Don't make phone calls while looking through racks of clothes or when a saleswoman is ringing you up. You are more likely to be impolite to other shoppers while talking on the phone, and the person on the other end will not get your full attention.

Apply lipstick, powder your nose, brush your hair, spray perfume, and perform any other beauty touchups in the **bathroom only.**

Stay home if you have a cold. It's no fun to be out shopping at your favorite boutique and have the woman next to you coughing or blowing her nose. Wait for your bug to pass before heading out—everyone will thank you.

Wearing an item you've bought and then returning it is **dishonest**, not to mention **totally tacky**. Once you remove the tags and wear your new clothes for more than just checking yourself out in the mirror, they are yours to keep.

"We are all born charming, fresh and
spontaneous, and must be civilized
before we are fit to participate in society."
—AMERICAN ETIQUETTE MAVEN MISS MANNERS

Etiquette Then ...

"In society it is etiquette for ladies
to have the best chairs and get handed things.
In home the reverse is the case. That is why
ladies are more sociable than gentlemen."
—VIRGINIA GRAHAM, MANNERS MAVEN

"Women are simply going to have to take over this world and that's all there is to it. All men want to do is start wars and show off in front of each other . . . most of them don't get past age twelve."
—MOTHER IN *STANDING IN THE RAINBOW*

and Now

"I can't stand seeing a mature woman walking around a department store or having lunch with her girlfriends wearing blue jeans."
—RUTH L. KERN, INTERNATIONAL ETIQUETTE CONSULTANT

The Glamorous Gabors

These classy dames knew how to live, love, and keep secrets.

The famous Gabor sisters—Zsa Zsa, Eva, and Magda—loved to be coy about their ages. At one point in her life, Zsa Zsa produced a birth certificate that said she was born in 1928, which would have had her married to her first husband at age eight. All three sisters were equally secretive; Eva's tombstone only gives her date of death, not birth. Notes the famous gossip columnist Cindy Adams about them: "I used to say that the only way you could tell the true age of a Gabor was by the rings around their gums."

Zsa Zsa and Eva looked so alike that even those who knew them well confused them. Once, when Eva was caught swimming nude in her pool by a telephone repairman, she pretended to be Zsa Zsa.

Between them,
the much-marrying
three sisters had
twenty husbands.

On Matters
of the
Heart

"It doesn't matter what you do in the
bedroom as long as you don't do it
in the street and frighten the horses."
—BRITISH ACTRESS MRS. PATRICK CAMPBELL. *At the turn
of the century, safe sex was much, much simpler.*

♥

"Lead me not into temptation;
I can find the way myself."
—RITA MAE BROWN

♥

"A girl can wait for the right man to
come along, but in the meantime that still
doesn't mean she can't have a wonderful
time with all the wrong ones."
—CHER

"French kissing is a mortal sin."

—CHERYL MURPHY DURZY'S MOTHER

The Lowdown
on Lip Locks—How to Be
Appropriate in Public

Throughout parts of the East, hand kissing is the custom. This is a practice in which you kiss your own hand, then press it against the forehead of the other person. (Much less germ-laden.)

Kissing in public was considered quite offensive in the early days of the United States. In 1656, a Bostonian was placed in the stocks for kissing his wife on the streets. And there are still laws on the books around the country that prohibit kissing. For instance, don't kiss a stranger in Cedar Rapids, Iowa; you could land in the clinker. And men with mustaches are not allowed to "habitually kiss human beings" in Indiana.

I Do, I Do Quiz

Being in a bridal party isn't only about wearing a goofy dress. Everyone has a job to do, but—according to Emily Post—
WHO DOES WHAT?

1. Makes the first toast at the reception

_____

2. Holds the bride's bouquet at the ceremony

_____

3. Escorts the groom's mother to her seat

_____

4. Pays for the bride's wedding ring

_____

5. Pays for the bride's gown

_____

6. Organizes a bridal shower

_____

7. Pays for the honeymoon

_____

8. Holds the bride's ring during the ceremony

_____

9. Escorts the bride up the aisle

_____

10. Stands first in the receiving line

_____

Answers on next page.

answers to I Do, I Do

1. Best man.
2. Maid of honor.
3. Head usher.
4. Groom.
5. Bride.
6. Bridesmaids.
7. Groom's family.
8. Best man.
9. Father of the bride.
10. Mother of the bride.

8—10 correct: I do
4—7 correct: I might
1—3 correct: I don't

"Marry a man younger than you and he will always keep you young at heart."

—AN AGELESS MOM

Gift Symbology

Looking to give a gift with meaning? According to the fascinating book, *The Language of Gifts*, virtually anything one could buy is loaded with symbolism. Here are some symbols that work especially well for women:

BASKETS: Women's domain; fertility; wholeness and togetherness

BROOMS: Female magic; domesticity; the contributions of wise women

SHELLS: The womb; fertility; resurrection

CAMELLIA: A unique woman; loveliness; excellence

VULTURE: Exemplary motherhood

UNICORN: Femininity; purity; goodness

THE NUMBER 4: Womanhood; root of all things; security; potential

EMILY POST
on Proper Fashion, circa 1922

"What makes a brilliant party? Clothes. Good clothes. A frumpy party is nothing more nor less than a collection of badly dressed persons."

"Rather be frumpy than vulgar! . . . Frumps are often celebrities in disguise—but a person of vulgar appearance is vulgar all through."

It's important to be chic, said she.
"*Chic* is a borrowed adjective, but there
is no English word to take the place
of elegant, which was destroyed utterly
by the reporter or practical joker who
said 'elegant dresses' ... "

"Fashion ought to be likened to a tide or
epidemic; sometimes one might define
it as a sort of hypnotism, seemingly
exerted by the gods as a joke."

Mind Your Manners:
A Quiz

Are you more familiar with fine dining or fast food? This test will tell, as you decide whether these rules of the table are in "perfect taste" or a "recipe for disaster."

1. The dessert fork should be placed above the dinner plate.

    Perfect taste   Recipe for disaster

2. It is acceptable to eat asparagus using your fingers.

    Perfect taste   Recipe for disaster

3. Cut your entire steak into small pieces before your first bite.

    Perfect taste   Recipe for disaster

4. Wait staff should always serve diners from the right.

    Perfect taste   Recipe for disaster

5. If you burp at the table, don't draw attention to yourself by saying "excuse me."
    Perfect taste   Recipe for disaster

6. At a formal dinner party, a woman should not be seated next to her husband or companion.
    Perfect taste   Recipe for disaster

7. Salad may be properly served after the main course.
    Perfect taste   Recipe for disaster

8. It is acceptable to blow on your soup to cool it.
    Perfect taste   Recipe for disaster

9. If you bite into a piece of bone or gristle, just chew and swallow like nothing is wrong.
    Perfect taste   Recipe for disaster

10. Your red wine glass has a relatively short stem and a rounded bowl.
    Perfect taste   Recipe for disaster

Answers on next page.

answers to
Mind Your Manners

1. **PERFECT TASTE.** The dessert fork and spoon will be placed horizontally above the dinner plate.

2. **PERFECT TASTE.** If the asparagus is served al dente— slightly firm to the bite.

3. **RECIPE FOR DISASTER.** Eat steak and other meats by cutting one small piece at a time.

4. **RECIPE FOR DISASTER.** Wait staff should always serve diners from the left and clear from the right.

5. **RECIPE FOR DISASTER.** Cover your mouth delicately when you burp at the table, and always excuse yourself—quietly.

6. **PERFECT TASTE.** A couple generally is not seated side-by-side at formal dinner parties.

7. **PERFECT TASTE.** There's nothing wrong with serving salad after the main course.

8. **RECIPE FOR DISASTER.** If it's too hot to eat, wait patiently until it cools. Never blow on it!

9. **RECIPE FOR DISASTER.** Besides being gross, swallowing bone or gristle is a good way to make yourself sick. Emily Post says you should remove it from your mouth as inconspicuously as possible using your fork. Then place it at the side of your plate.

10. **PERFECT TASTE.** Red wine glasses are bowled so that the warmth of your hand reaches the wine when you hold the glass.

8—10 correct: Perfect guest
4—7 correct: Well-mannered
1—3 correct: Elbows off the table!

Rules to Live
by for the
"Perfect Lady"

"Nothing is less important
than which fork you use."
—EMILY POST, the perfect lady

"If you obey all the rules
you miss all the fun."
—KATHARINE HEPBURN

"If you can't be a good example,
then you'll just have to be
a horrible warning."
—CATHERINE AIRD, author of witty
British police novels

> **"Answer me! Don't talk with food in your mouth!"** —ERMA BOMBECK'S MOTHER

When in China...

Manners vary across the globe. For example, in China, although folks tend to eat three meals a day, the distinction between breakfast, lunch, and dinner foods is not the same as in other parts of the world; rather, the types of food served at the three meals is pretty much the same.

Napkins are not traditionally used. Instead, diners are given a hot towel at the end of the meal to clean their hands and faces.

❖

People begin eating according to age, with the oldest person starting first, then the next oldest, ending with the youngest.

❖

It is considered incredibly rude to leave anything on your plate, even one grain.

❖

No liquids except soup tend to be served during meals. Tea is drunk separately throughout the day.

Helpful Hints from Mommie Dearest, JOAN CRAWFORD

"It's an insult to a guest to offer meat on a plate that's come right out of the cupboard. It should be heated first."

"Sit on hard chairs— soft ones spread the hips."

To avoid a nasty surprise, "always pack in daylight."

"Regular exercise, all alone, can be boring . . . Get all those pleasingly plump pals together *regularly* at a certain hour on certain days of the week—and compete."

And as for posture, she told women to "get their shoulders back where God meant them to be."

HEADS UP:
Hair Tips

"To get soft hair, collect rainwater in a barrel and use it for rinsing."

—ALICIA ALVREZ'S MOTHER

"If you see someone with a stunning haircut, grab her by the wrist and demand fiercely to know the name, address, and home phone number of her hairdresser. If she refuses to tell you, burst into tears."
—CYNTHIA HEIMEL

"Never let your left hand know what your right hand is doing."

—ODETTE CLAYTON CHARBONET

Fingernail Facts

If you are less than happy about the state of your nails, remember that the fashion of long, perfect nails developed among wealthy ladies of leisure who had not much else to do with their time than to spend it having their nails done.

⊙

It is the fashion in many countries to grow one fingernail to show you don't have to do manual labor. Which nail it is varies—in the Philippines it's the thumbnail; in Greece it's the pinky.

⊙

Ancient Egyptians, ahead in this as in so many things, were one of the first people to use fingernail polish—they would color their nails with henna.

priceless advice from
EMILY POST

Since in Ms. Post's estimation freckles are the very worst thing that can happen to a woman (calling them "as violent as they are hideous"), she counsels wearing an orange-red veil when out in the sun.

✳

Because of the vulgarity of most exercise outfits, "the young woman who wants to look pretty should confine her exercise to dancing. She can also hold a parasol over her head and sit in a canoe."

"You must never wear an evening dress and a hat!"

"One should always wear a simpler dress in one's own house than one wears in going to the house of another."

✳

"Elderly women should not wear grass green, or royal blue, or purple....Pink and orchid are often very becoming to older women.... Because a woman is no longer young is no reason why she should wear perpetual black—unless she is fat."

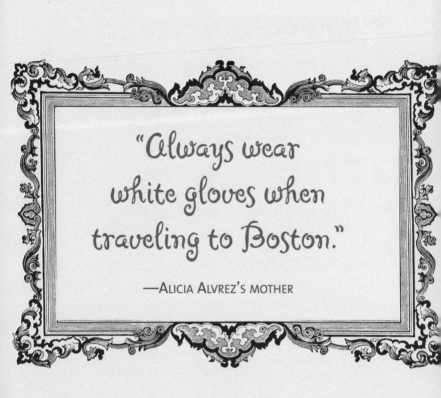

"Always wear
white gloves when
traveling to Boston."

—ALICIA ALVREZ'S MOTHER

Eat It or Wear It?

Some you eat and some you wear. Which is which?

1. Obi   Eat it   Wear it
2. Nori   Eat it   Wear it
3. Sake   Eat it   Wear it
4. Sari   Eat it   Wear it
5. Chanterelle   Eat it   Wear it
6. Chamomile   Eat it   Wear it
7. Chasuble   Eat it   Wear it
8. Cherimoya   Eat it   Wear it
9. Balaclava   Eat it   Wear it
10. Baklava   Eat it   Wear it

Answers on next page.

1. WEAR IT. An OBI is the sash used to bind a Japanese kimono.

2. EAT IT. NORI is the edible, dried seaweed used to wrap sushi.

3. EAT IT. Actually, drink it. SAKE is Japanese wine made from fermented rice.

4. WEAR IT. A SARI is the traditional garment worn by Hindu women.

5. EAT IT. CHANTERELLES are bright yellow or orange wild mushrooms.

6. EAT IT. CHAMOMILE flowers look like daisies and are dried and used in tea.

7. WEAR IT. A CHASUBLE is the sleeveless tunic worn over the priest's robe during Mass.

8. EAT IT. CHERIMOYAS are also known as custard apples.

9. WEAR IT. A BALACLAVA is a close-fitting knitted hood that covers the head, ears, and neck, leaving only the face exposed.

10. EAT IT. BAKLAVA is a sweet pastry from Greece and Turkey, made with layers of phyllo dough and drenched in honey.

8—10 correct: Dressed for success
4—7 correct: Well dressed
1—3 correct: Is that what you're wearing?

"Words are the clothes you wear, and I know you want to be well dressed."
—NAOMI JUDD'S MOTHER

Culinary Tips

"The secret to making good bread is that there is no secret. Let your imagination help you break any rules you imagine exist to daunt you."

—JACQUELINE DEVAL

Well-Done

"How to eat [spinach] like a child: Divide into piles. Rearrange again into piles. After five or six maneuvers, sit back and say you are full."
—DELIA EPHRON

❋

"The cherry tomato is a wonderful invention, producing, as it does, a satisfactorily explosive squish when bitten."
—MISS MANNERS

❋

"COOKING TIP: Wrap turkey leftovers in aluminum foil and throw them out."
—NICOLE HOLLANDER

Grateful acknowledgment is made to the following for permission to reprint material copyrighted by them. All reprinted by permission of Red Wheel/Weiser.

Alicia Alvrez, *The Ladies' Room Reader*. Boston, MA: Conari Press, an imprint of Red Wheel/Weiser, 2000. On pages 14–15, 33, 38–39, 62–63.

Alicia Alvrez, *The Ladies' Room Reader Revisited*. Boston, MA: Conari Press, an imprint of Red Wheel/Weiser, 2002. On pages 20–23, 28–29, 40–41, 48–51, 55, 56–57.

Alicia Alvrez, *The Ladies' Room Reader Quiz Book*. Boston, MA: Conari Press, an imprint of Red Wheel/Weiser, 2004. On pages 34–36, 42–45, 59–61.

Alicia Alvrez, *Mama Says*. Boston, MA: Conari Press, an imprint of Red Wheel/Weiser, 2004. On pages 6, 17, 27, 32, 37, 48, 52, 54, 58, 61.

Ame Mahler Beanland and Emily Miles Terry, *It's a Chick Thing*. Boston, MA: Conari Press, an imprint of Red Wheel/Weiser, 2000. On pages 7, 8–10, 12–13, 18–19, 53.

Amanda Ford, *Retail Therapy*. Boston, MA: Conari Press, an imprint of Red Wheel/Weiser, 2002. On pages 24–25.

BJ Gallagher, *Everything I Need to Know I Learned from Other Women*. Boston, MA: Conari Press, an imprint of Red Wheel/Weiser, 2002. On pages 17, 47.

Autumn Stephens, *Out of the Mouths of Babes*. Boston, MA: Conari Press, an imprint of Red Wheel/Weiser, 2000. On pages 26, 47.

Autumn Stephens, *Wild Words from Wild Women*. Boston, MA: Conari Press, an imprint of Red Wheel/Weiser, 1993. On pages 16, 26, 31.